THIS BOOK BELONGS TO:

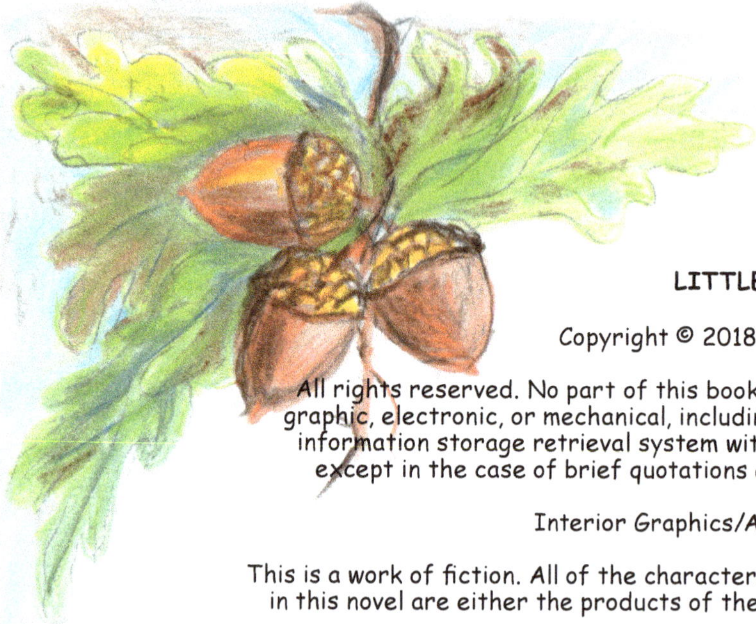

iUniverse books may be ordered through booksellers or by contacting:

iUniverse
1663 Liberty Drive
Bloomington, IN 47403
www.iuniverse.com
1-800-Authors (1-800-288-4677)

ISBN: 978-1-5320-4628-5 (sc)
ISBN: 978-1-5320-4629-2 (e)

Library of Congress Control Number: 2018904192

Print information available on the last page.

iUniverse rev. date: 04/26/2018

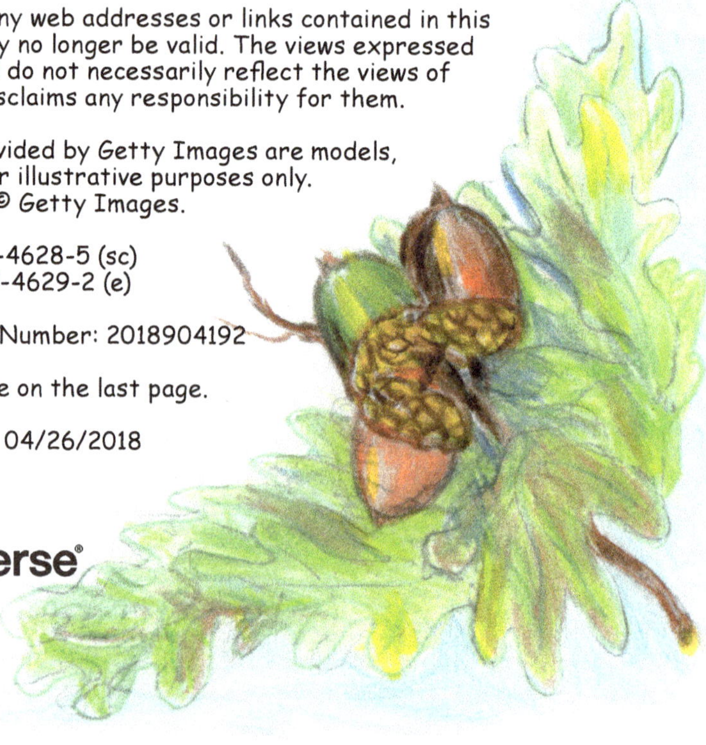

LITTLE ACORN

Written by Ann Jeter Baldwin
Illustrations by Jack Jeter

LISTEN

LOOK

LEARN

LITTLE ACORN

Dedicated to Ava Rose Baldwin
and all curious children

Written by Ann Jeter Baldwin
Illustrations by Jack Jeter

Sis and Bro Publishing Company
Norfolk, Virginia

I'm a little acorn that fell upon the ground.

I am so smooth and round and brown.

Do you think I can grow by leaps and bounds?

I want to be the tallest tree in town.

When I'm new my shell is a glorious green.

It's the loveliest color you've ever seen.

I'm wearing a cap when I fall from the tree

Because it helps me stick there before I'm free.

I'm a little acorn that wants to grow tall

But maybe I'm just a little too small.

I'm a little acorn that can't fly or crawl.

It seems I can do nothing at all.

The squirrels and birds come around for a treat.

They think I am something tasty to eat.

I'm full of stuff that's good for their tummy.

They gobble me up because I'm so yummy.

I'm a little acorn that might stick in the dirt.

I could even get a great growth spurt.

My shell will crack open and not even hurt.

Have you seen such a thing coming
out of the earth?

Look around in the yard and the flower garden.

You may find me where I have been forgotten

Growing a crooked stem and a few wavy leaves.

Now I'm looking as perky as can be.

I'm a little acorn that may become an oak tree.

I'm a little acorn that could be tall as can be.

I'm a little acorn that can grow big limbs and leaves.

That little acorn just might be ME!

Acorns
to
Oak Trees

Now that you know more than you did before

about little acorns and large oak trees,

here are some **fun facts** for you to explore.

Did you know?

Acorns are seeds and nuts that grow on oak trees.

Only one in 10,000 acorns becomes an oak tree.

Acorns take between 6 to 20 months before a new tree begins to sprout.

The colors, shapes and sizes of acorns depend on the type of their mother oak trees.

The acorn is a symbol of long life and good luck.

Acorns drop from the oak trees in the fall.

Acorns are good food for animals like
squirrels, deer and even birds.

Acorns can also make some animals
sick like dogs and horses.

Some people eat roasted acorns.

Acorns can be ground to make flour and coffee.

There are 600 types of oak trees and
some can live over 600 years.

Oak trees can grow to 70 feet high
and 9 feet wide.

Oak trees start making acorns when they
are 20 to 50 years old.

One oak tree can produce more than
2,000 acorns each year.

Oak trees can take in 50 gallons of groundwater (a bath tubful) every day through their roots.

Oak wood is very strong and very hard.

Oak wood is used to make furniture, houses and many other useful things.

The oak tree has been named "America's Tree."

Color us ...